First Facts

REALLY SCARY STUFF

SCARY MONSTERS

by Jim Whiting

Consultant:
Elizabeth Tucker
Professor of English
Binghamton University
Binghamton, New York

CAPSTONE PRESS
a capstone imprint

First Facts is published by Capstone Press,
151 Good Counsel Drive, P.O. Box 669, Mankato, Minnesota 56002.
www.capstonepress.com

092009
005618CGS10

 Books published by Capstone Press are manufactured with paper
containing at least 10 percent post-consumer waste.

Library of Congress Cataloging-in-Publication Data
Whiting, Jim, 1951–
    Scary monsters / by Jim Whiting.
    p. cm. — (First Facts, really scary stuff)
    Includes bibliographical references and index.
    Summary:"Describes stories about monsters and explores whether monsters
exist or not"— Provided by publisher.
    ISBN 978-1-4296-3968-2 (library binding)
    1. Monsters — Juvenile literature. 2. Animals, Mythical — Juvenile literature. I. Title.
GR825.W43 2010
398.24'54 — dc22   2009023386

Editorial Credits

Jennifer Besel, editor; Alison Thiele, designer; Marcie Spence, media researcher;
    Eric Manske, production specialist

Photo Credits

Fortean Picture Library, 16; Getty Images Inc./Tom Stoddart, 8; Hammer/The Kobal Collection,
15; Kolonics, Istvan/Private Collection/The Bridgeman Art Library International, 20; Newscom,
6; Newscom/Andy Holzman, 18; Paul Mudie, 12; Shutterstock/ChipPix, 21; Shutterstock/
Colman Lerner Garardo, 11; Shutterstock/Denisenko, cover; Shutterstock/Margaret M Stewart, 5;
Shutterstock/Natasha R. Graham, throughout (green background); Shutterstock/Volkova Anna,
throughout (spooky background)

**The legends and stories presented in this book may have different versions. The versions used
in this book are considered by researchers to be the most common telling of the event or story.**

TABLE OF CONTENTS

AHHH! Is That Thing Real? 4

Lurking in the Lake 7

Brain-Eating Monsters 10

Monsters in the Moonlight 13

Mummy's Curse 14

Huge, Hairy, and Horrible! 17

Bloodsuckers 20

Glossary 22

Read More 23

Internet Sites 23

Index 24

AHHH! IS THAT THING REAL?

For thousands of years, people have told stories about scary monsters. Legends tell of monsters that rise from the dead to eat brains. Other stories describe a snakelike monster that slithers through a murky lake. But are these monsters real? Let's look at six scary creatures. You decide if they are real or not.

legend — an old story that could be believable

Some people believe this photo proves the Loch Ness monster is real. Others believe this picture is a fake.

LURKING IN THE LAKE

The cold, dark waters of Scotland's Loch Ness hold a mystery. Some people believe they have seen a monster swimming there. They call the creature Nessie.

Some say Nessie has a thin neck and snakelike body. Others say the monster has horns or a long tail.

loch — a lake

Scientists looked for the Loch Ness monster. Using **sonar**, scientists tracked an object. The object was bigger than anything known to live in the lake. Could that be Nessie?

sonar — an instrument used to find underwater objects

FACT or FICTION

Is There a Strange Creature in Loch Ness?

Yes People have reported sightings of the Loch Ness monster for hundreds of years.

Yes People have taken pictures of something that looks like a strange creature.

Yes Loch Ness is more than 800 feet (244 meters) deep. A large creature could easily hide in the deep water.

No People have different descriptions of Nessie. They could be making up their reports.

No Some pictures of the creature have been proven to be fake. Other pictures are too blurry to tell for sure what is shown.

No From a distance, people might mistake a log or an eel for a monster.

BRAIN-EATING MONSTERS

Watch your step near cemeteries. Stories say that the dead can come back to life as zombies. According to legends, zombies can't think or feel pain. They only live to eat tasty human brains.

Scary movies show zombies with slimy, rotting bodies.

MONSTERS IN THE MOONLIGHT

Be careful when the full moon is out! Stories say people turn into werewolves under the full moon. Thick fur sprouts from their bodies. They grow fangs and sharp claws.

Terrifying howls could mean a werewolf is hunting. Werewolves are said to rip people apart for a midnight snack. At dawn, werewolves change back into humans. Yikes!

MUMMY'S CURSE

Long ago, Egyptian kings were wrapped in cloth and buried in tombs. These royal mummies were buried with piles of treasure.

Some people believe a mummy's treasure is cursed. If its treasure is disturbed, the mummy will rise to life. It will kill anyone who dares to take its riches.

tomb — a room for holding a dead body
cursed — affected by an evil spell

HUGE, HAIRY, AND HORRIBLE!

Does a huge, hairy monster live deep in the forest? Many hikers say they have spotted a hairy monster called Bigfoot. Reports describe Bigfoot as part human and part ape. People say it gives off a terrible smell. With an estimated weight of 500 pounds (227 kilograms), Bigfoot is a scary monster indeed. That is, if it is real.

This famous photo has made many people believe Bigfoot is real. But other people think it's just a person in a costume.

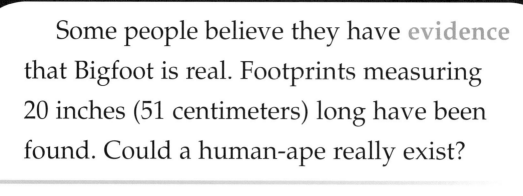

Some people believe they have evidence that Bigfoot is real. Footprints measuring 20 inches (51 centimeters) long have been found. Could a human-ape really exist?

evidence — information that helps prove something is true or false

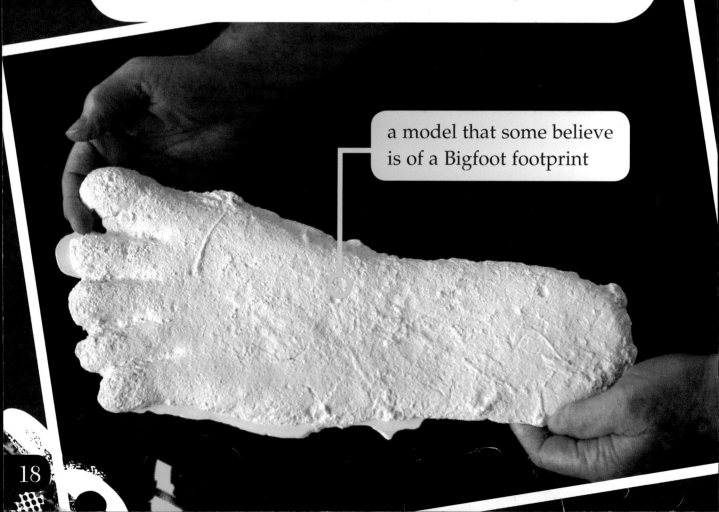

a model that some believe is of a Bigfoot footprint

FACT or FICTION

Does Bigfoot Really Exist?

Yes People have found footprints and hair near Bigfoot sightings. The hair and prints don't match any known animal.

Yes Some people have taken fuzzy pictures of a hairy creature. There is even a film.

Yes Bigfoot could be an animal that scientists haven't yet discovered.

No Some people have dressed in gorilla costumes for fake pictures. Others have made fake footprints.

No Bigfoot stories have been around a long time. Yet no one has ever found a body or bones.

No Bears standing on their hind legs could look like hairy monsters.

BLOODSUCKERS

Legends say vampires live on human blood. Vampires bite their **victims'** throats with sharp fangs. Then they suck out the hot, sticky blood.

victim — a person who is hurt or killed

It is said that vampires return to their coffins after they feast. They sleep during the day. They wake to feed each night.

Are vampires or any monsters real? You'll have to decide. But you may want to keep the lights on just in case.

GLOSSARY

cursed (KURSD) — affected by an evil spell

evidence (EV-uh-duhns) — information, items, and facts that help prove something is true or false

legend (LEJ-uhnd) — a story handed down from earlier times that could seem believable

loch (LAHK) — a lake

sonar (SOH-nar) — an instrument used to figure out how deep water is or where underwater objects are

tomb (TOOM) — a grave or room for holding a dead body

victim (VIK-tuhm) — a person who is hurt, killed, or made to suffer

READ MORE

Besel, Jennifer M. *Vampires.* Monsters. Mankato, Minn.: Capstone Press, 2007.

Penner, Lucille Recht. *Monsters.* A Stepping Stone Book. New York: Random House, 2009.

Wallace, Holly. *The Mystery of the Loch Ness Monster.* Can Science Solve? Chicago: Heinemann, 2006.

INTERNET SITES

FactHound offers a safe, fun way to find Internet sites related to this book. All of the sites on FactHound have been researched by our staff.

Here's all you do:

Visit *www.facthound.com*

FactHound will fetch the best sites for you!

INDEX

Bigfoot, 17–19
brains, 4, 10

coffins, 21
curses, 14

footprints, 18, 19
full moon, 13

Loch Ness monster, 4, 6,
    7–9

mummies, 14

scientists, 8, 19
sonar, 8

tombs, 14
treasure, 14

vampires, 20–21

werewolves, 13

zombies, 10